Fast and Slow

Julie Murray

Abdo Kids Junior
is an Imprint of Abdo Kids
abdobooks.com

Abdo
OPPOSITES
Kids

abdobooks.com

Published by Abdo Kids, a division of ABDO, P.O. Box 398166, Minneapolis, Minnesota 55439.
Copyright © 2019 by Abdo Consulting Group, Inc. International copyrights reserved in all countries.
No part of this book may be reproduced in any form without written permission from the publisher.
Abdo Kids Junior™ is a trademark and logo of Abdo Kids.

Printed in the United States of America, North Mankato, Minnesota.

102018

012019

THIS BOOK CONTAINS
RECYCLED MATERIALS

Photo Credits: iStock, Shutterstock

Production Contributors: Teddy Borth, Jennie Forsberg, Grace Hansen

Design Contributors: Christina Doffing, Candice Keimig, Dorothy Toth

Library of Congress Control Number: 2018946162

Publisher's Cataloging-in-Publication Data

Names: Murray, Julie, author.

Title: Fast and slow / by Julie Murray.

Description: Minneapolis, Minnesota : Abdo Kids, 2019 | Series: Opposites |
     Includes glossary, index and online resources (page 24).

Identifiers: ISBN 9781532181788 (lib. bdg.) | ISBN 9781532182761 (ebook) |
     ISBN 9781532183256 (Read-to-me ebook)

Subjects: LCSH: Synonyms and antonyms--Juvenile literature. | Polarity--Juvenile
     literature. | Locomotion--Juvenile literature. | Kinetics--Juvenile literature.

Classification: DDC 428.1--dc23

Table of Contents

Fast and Slow

A motorcycle is fast. It can go more than 100 mph (161 kph).

A tricycle is slow.

Joe learns to ride.

A cheetah is fast. It can run up to 75 mph (121 kph).

A sloth is slow. It is the slowest **mammal**.

A car goes fast.

A race car can go

200 mph (322 kph).

A tractor goes slow.

It works in the **field**.

A mako shark is fast. It can swim 60 mph (96.5 kph)!

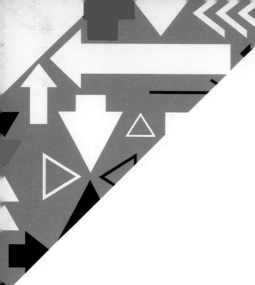

A seahorse swims slow. It is the slowest fish in the sea.

Look around you. What do you see that moves fast? What do you see that moves slow?

More Things Fast and Slow

butterfly

inline skating

space shuttle

caterpillar

crawling

hot air balloon

Glossary

field
a wide area of open land often used for growing crops.

mammal
a warm-blooded animal with fur on its skin. Mother mammals make milk for their babies.

Index

Abdo Kids
ONLINE
FREE! ONLINE MULTIMEDIA RESOURCES

Visit **abdokids.com** and use this code to access crafts, games, videos, and more!

Abdo Kids Code:
OFK1788

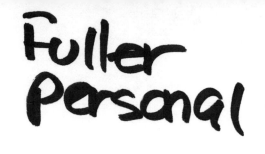

Fuller
Personal